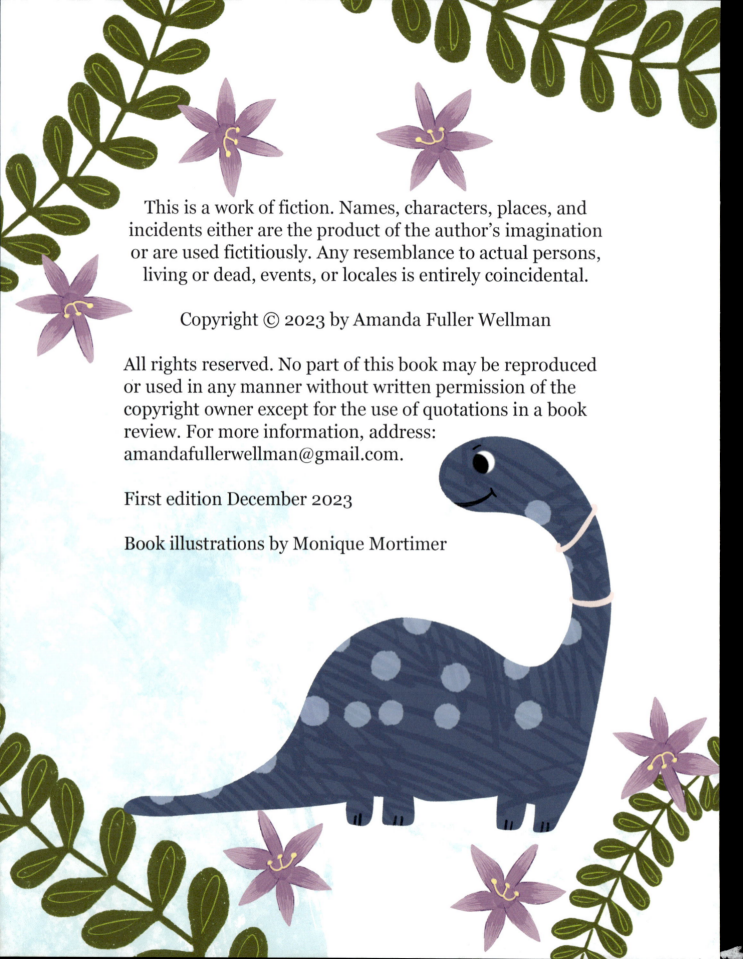

This is a work of fiction. Names, characters, places, and incidents either are the product of the author's imagination or are used fictitiously. Any resemblance to actual persons, living or dead, events, or locales is entirely coincidental.

Copyright © 2023 by Amanda Fuller Wellman

All rights reserved. No part of this book may be reproduced or used in any manner without written permission of the copyright owner except for the use of quotations in a book review. For more information, address: amandafullerwellman@gmail.com.

First edition December 2023

Book illustrations by Monique Mortimer

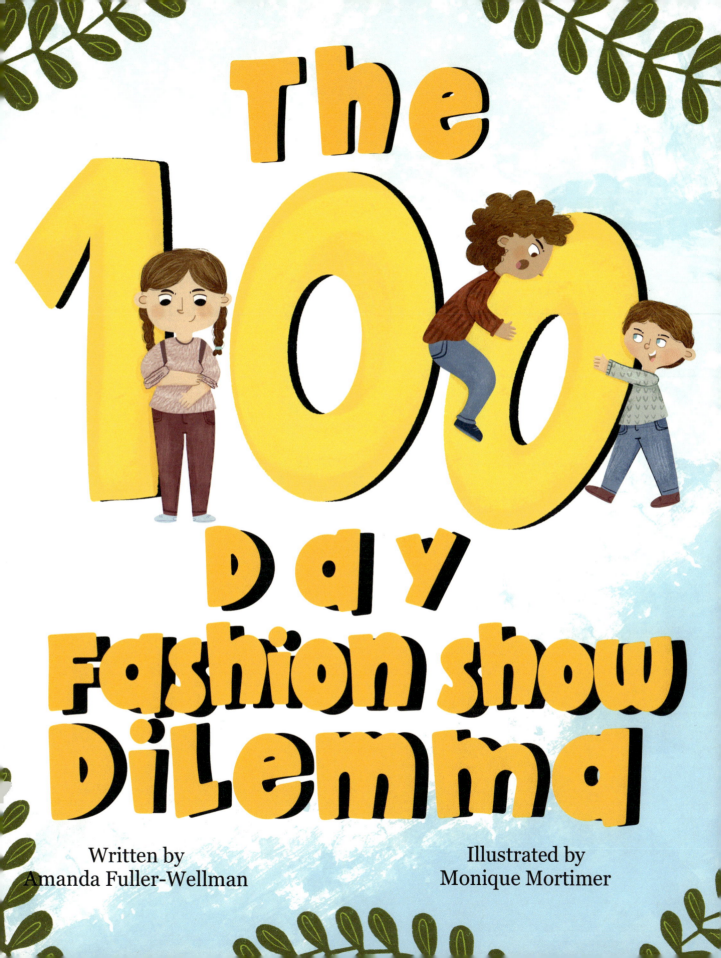

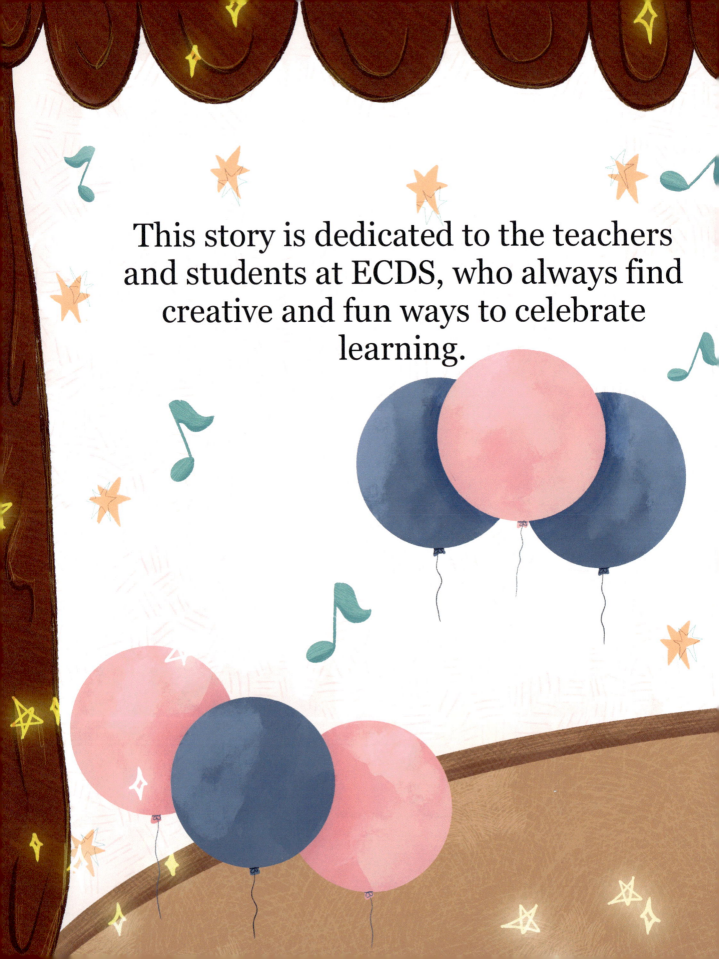

This story is dedicated to the teachers and students at ECDS, who always find creative and fun ways to celebrate learning.

We are Winnie, Ike and Zavier.
The W.I.Z. Kids
The problem-solving trio here to help.

We are a sibling group of three.
We help solve problems that we see.

Along with our group is our curious dog Wonder.
We can solve any problem-North, East, West, and Down Under.

We are known best as the W. I. Z. Kids and Wonder, our dog.
Solving dilemmas, finding a clear path through the fog.

W.I.Z and Wonder: Wonder and W.I.Z.

Now that you know who we are,
Join us as we solve our latest challenge so far.

Winnie, Ike , and Zavier were about to join the school for the 100 day event. It was a celebration of 100 days of school and Kindergarten was to represent.

However, as the three siblings were about to sit down, the kindergarten teacher pulled them aside with a frown.

She quickly explained that four students were short the 100 things they need.
She asked the problem-solving trio if they could help. Of course, they agreed.

The teacher said,
"Leo has 90 spiders and is missing the last 10.
Val has 80 flowers and needs 20 more to begin.

Ezra has 70 dinosaurs, but is short the 30 other,
Maribel has 60 rubber bands, but still needs 40 from her mother.

Winnie knew almost immediately,
That they would have to gather these 100 items expediently*.

To Zavier and Ike, Winnie said, "Remember 10 is our best friend.
If we find the items 10 at a time this problem we will quickly mend.

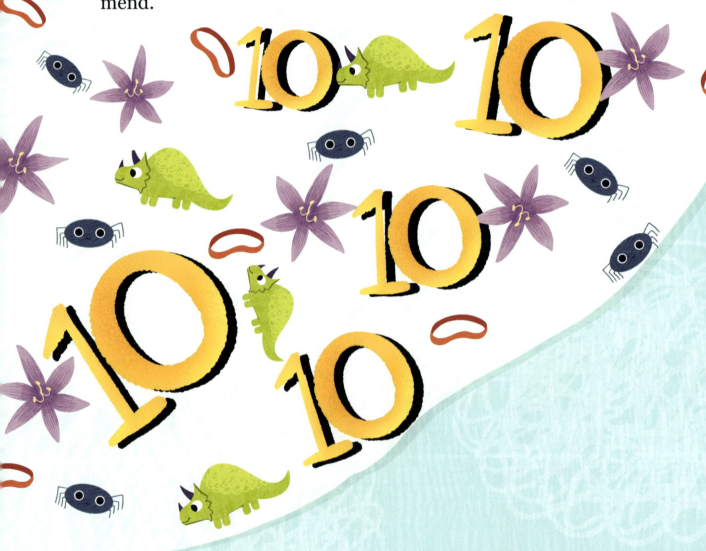

*Expediently: quickly and orderly

"Let's start with the spiders," Ike said, "Leo only needs ten.

Our first friend, ten can be found in the old Halloween storage den."

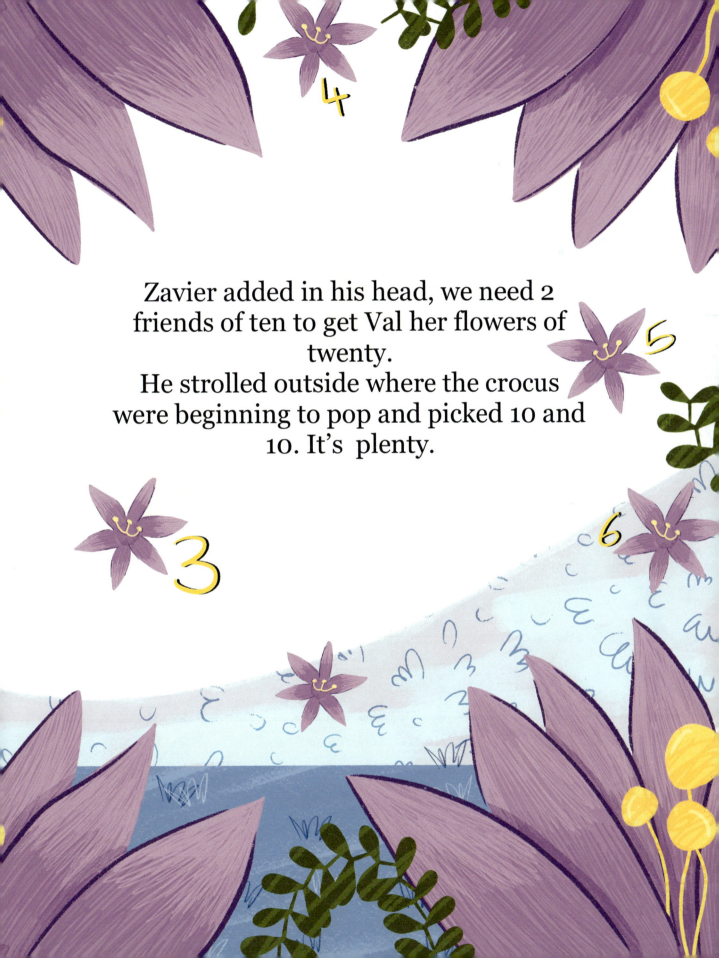

Zavier added in his head, we need 2 friends of ten to get Val her flowers of twenty.
He strolled outside where the crocus were beginning to pop and picked 10 and 10. It's plenty.

The sibling trio knew 10 spiders and 20 flowers makes 3 tens, which, so far, is thirty.

7 tens more will complete the job. The three rolled up their sleeves, realizing they may get dirty.

We have 30 and need 70 more.
Let's see if Maribel's mother is at the door.

Yay!! She was there with her 40 rubber bands. That is 4 tens to add.

Us three don't have enough hands.

We were in the final stretch.
Our last 30 items were some dinosaurs to fetch.

We paced and we paced back and forth on the school floor.

Until Ike proclaimed, "Let's go to the sandbox and explore!"

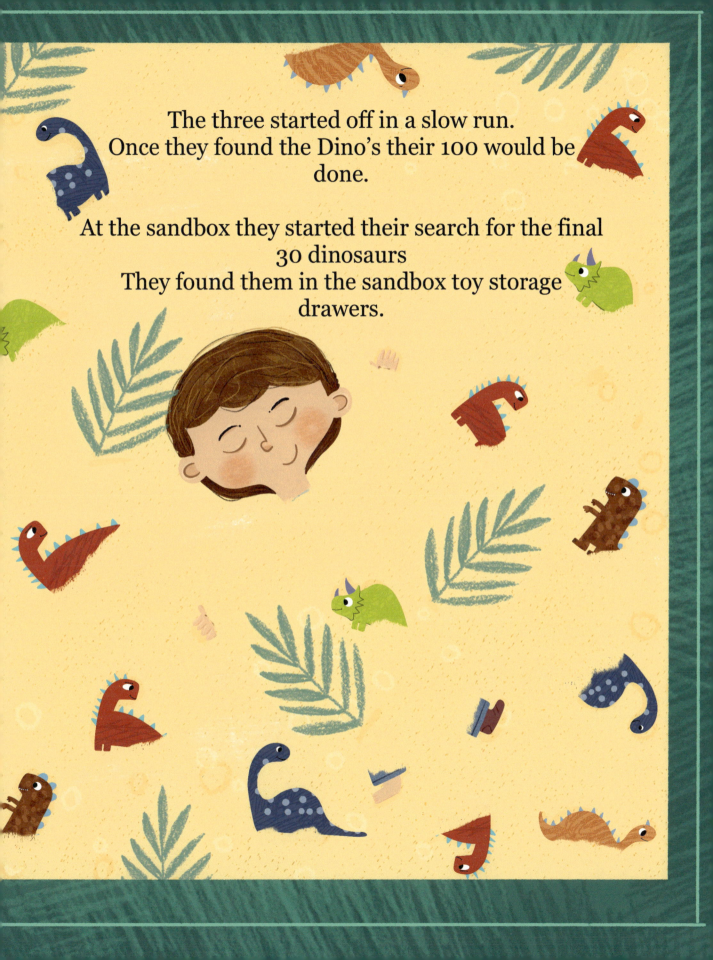

The three started off in a slow run.
Once they found the Dino's their 100 would be done.

At the sandbox they started their search for the final 30 dinosaurs
They found them in the sandbox toy storage drawers.

The three raced back to the assembly as quick as they could.

They showed the kindergarten teacher their findings.

She gave a big smile, as they knew she would.

She gathered the final 100 items and passed them to the students in need.

They attached them to their 100 day Fashion gear with speed.

The siblings hastily took their seats in the gym. Just as the fashion show was about to begin.

In their heads, the trio did a quick review, of all the adding they had had to do.

Leo had needed 10, Val 20, Ezra needed 30, and Maribel needed 40 things.

The three quietly thought of how they found the 100 for them and felt like kings.

The music had started and the students were walking down the runway
A happy ending to what had started as a hectic day.

Activity Page

Author

Amanda Fuller-Wellman is a learning support teacher for students in K-8 grades. She has been writing short stories for many years and is excited to begin to share them. Amanda lives in Colorado with her family and their dog

Illustrator

Monique Mortimer is a qualified social worker with experience in early childhood development. She can always be found drawing fun and quirky characters or reading murder mystery novels. Monique lives in Port Elizabeth, South Africa.